THIS HOUSE

THIS HOUSE

Poems by Rehema Njambi

For the women I love, who have
modelled strength in adversity.

છ્ક

THE EMMA PRESS

First published in the UK in 2021 by The Emma Press Ltd.
Poems © Rehema Njambi 2021.

All rights reserved.

The right of Rehema Njambi to be identified as the author of
this work has been asserted in accordance with the Copyright,
Designs and Patents Act 1988.

ISBN 978-1-912915-72-9

A CIP catalogue record of this book
is available from the British Library.

Printed and bound in the UK
by the Holodeck, Birmingham.

The Emma Press
theemmapress.com
hello@theemmapress.com
Birmingham, UK

CONTENTS

All These Truths You Never Set Free

I reach for the pen and I remember
that you wanted this for yourself.

This selfishness of pen and paper and solitude,
hand gripped over muse's wrist.

Anything to keep this gift that you once had
but could not turn into anything.

All these truths you never set free
resting in the hands you gave to me.

Found Wanting

Offer up your arms and words of comfort

Say tomorrow will make it better, or it will be okay

Lay down and wrap yourself around her like this

Feel as lost as two people in a house can feel

Still you love / are loved/ will do anything for love

Offer up your dreams, your nights, your days

Tell anyone who asks that
You slept
You ate

The men in this house are always making you cry

The men in this house have carved their names on your face

Now you learn how inadequate your love really is

Your love does not really help or *do* anything

The men in this house are always making things hard

things hurt

things ache

(It's harder when you think about it)

their platitudes in place of hope.

Confession

We talk about the nature of glue:
animal bones and skins.
Being twenty-five and being glue –
changing atoms and molecules.
Being fourteen and being glue –
silent. Sealing secrets.

We talk about that time when she was five.
She drinks. Glass after glass after –
and I should stop her, but I can't.

She tells me about blood:
made up of liquid and solids.
Blood on hands and blood on thighs –
platelets, red blood cells, white blood cells.
Forgetting to burn the bloody rags.

She laughs when she remembers.
No one could have guessed it was her.
I took the biggest knife, she says,
steady hands curving round the black handle.
I pointed it at his bloated stomach
and told him: Out!

She reaches out for my hand. Holds tight.
She says, I don't want to be glue.

I put on silence when I leave.

Marriage Circa 1975

She asked her husband
if men ever got their periods
and was angry when he said no.

We laugh at how absurd,
how ridiculous it is to marry a man
when you do not even know that.

A Piece of Land

My mother's joy is tied to the ground;
to the earth.

She strives to have some of
what she is made of in her hands,
says belonging is only belonging
when you can root yourself
in the thing from which you are made.

Our fathers handed down belonging to their sons,
gave away their daughters,
said belonging is only belonging
when you can feed yourself
with the thing from which you are made.

*

'For you are dust and to dust you shall return…'
my grandmother tells me, and hands me a garden hoe.
She says no one knows what it is like to till land
that is not yours like a woman,
but belonging is only belonging
when you can touch the thing from which you are made.

Acres and acres stretch before us –
my people have always been farmers,
have known the rhythms of seed and harvest,
the weight of waiting for seasons to change,
the sweat of your brow growing what you will eat.

'Ngai akĩoya tĩĩri kuuma thĩ, akĩũmba mũndũ na tĩĩri ũcio…'
my grandfather tells me, and hands me a marigold.

He holds my hand and shows me all that is his
with the pride of a man that knows where he is seeded.
He says his roots will grow here, live and be sustained here,
and I am proud.

'Yet Each Man Kills The Thing He Loves'

When the letters came
I buried my head in the crook of my arms.

Then the phone calls.
They were harder to ignore.

Finally, the knock on the door
and I could not hide anymore
so I told you the truth.

A Lending, Not a Giving

Every haven you have ever found
was only lent to you.

Even now you abide in your body
like a stranger house-sitting for a friend of a friend

and with each new day
you set a reminder to remind me

that souls like yours do not
have a permanent residence.

Every moment of being with you
is a lesson that love is not enough.

In Holy Matrimony

You want Holiness,
purity served on a plate

with a sizeable portion of eagerness
and a side of demure.

All night you insist on a love,
a body so pure it is drenched

in myrrh, and frankincense, wrapped in gold
and anointed with oil that drips and drips

and soaks its essence into
the skin of your hands.

Your hands demand something holy to hold.
I am angry, and tired.

And I Am Angry Because

I gave you all my secrets
and they were not safe in your hands.

Because I was ready and you said wait.
I have grown roots in the place I was standing,

waiting. We could have made our way to your door,
kicked off the hesitation, taken off our aches

and made our way to the corner room
you showed me once.
We could have lived.

Our Marriage Dies in a Dream

I dream of your ancestors / your grandfather / beckoning me into the field / heart pounding / for he is dead / I know / I push my way through the field of corn /

Now reaching up to the sky / now shining gold in the sun / now standing by his side / now at the centre of the field /

This is not the place for you / he tells me / *We will eat your flesh and burn your bones to ash* /

In the morning / I wake / gasping / hands shaking / the smell of burning flesh chasing me out of my dream / I grab what I can and run.

Envy

There is my truth
living in another's mouth.

Dancing with ease on their tongue,
making a mockery of my silence.

Come back, I say. Come and be mine again
and I will be at home with you.

Ghosts In This House

There were footsteps in the dark all night,
almost every night, and we were scared
but we didn't say a thing.

She called us to prayer in the morning, every morning.
With our small hands and smaller faith

we asked the Lord for protection
but He didn't say a thing.

One Of Them

I think he thinks the Lord is at rest.
Eyes closed, feet strung up,
the sour smell of unused glory
and month-old litanies littering the temple –
he thinks the Lord will not see.

Deep down beneath the soil
the maggots are gathering,
satisfying themselves, feasting
on bodies smothered in dirt
and garnished with sin.

I think he thinks he will never be one of them,
but the blood is like ink on his hands –

washable, but the constant hint
of its presence… lingers.

He thinks the Lord will not see.

We Do Not Mend Broken Things

When you step into a room, every broken
thing we own scatters into the shadows
scrambling for a place to hide.

Even those that can still be loved
in their brokenness, we dare not touch.
The tilt of your head always leans in too close
to the lines we are trying to glue together.

As if so to say:
What a mockery of wholeness this is,
what a miserable exercise.

I Make Small Observances For You

Every now and then, I wake myself up
and make observances for you.

Head bowed, I pick a colour you would love,
drape it round my neck and make
my way to the graveyard.

I bring you the phrases you loved,
cradled in flowers you would loathe
for their soft willingness to live.

I lay them at the mouth of your door,
these *'no one wants you*'s
and these *'you're better off dead*'s.

Oleander, aconitum. Carolina Jessamine.
All to remind you that I buried you, and it was good.

Ihoya

Feed me your truth.
Feed me like you would a starved stray
that has crawled to your door:
with hands outstretched,
mercy at the ready,
body hidden in the shadows
between the open door and the wall
in case I am feral
and need to be tamed.

Vigil for Loneliness

Solitude
> *synonym, synonym*
Sleeping eight to a room,
> *antonym, antonym*

I own nothing for myself.

When the morning goes
> *antonym, antonym*
I find myself thinking:
> *synonym, synonym*

This synonym does not work.

Prayer on My Mother's Tongue

is holy revival in a Pentecostal church on Easter Sunday.
The choir's hands raised as *Hallelujah!* strips its way
through the too-British reticence,
because Sundays –
Sundays are for the highest praise.
Our best clothes dirty and wrinkled as we roll on the floor;
shoes scuffed, or lost, a pair of heels abandoned at the altar
as the sound of the drumbeat and tambourine
stirs up a shout, a dance we move along to
as we stamp our feet and clap our hands –
the laying on of hands and worship lasts as long
as the Lord is willing to linger and grace us with Presence.
On Sundays my mother's prayer is all it can be:
a cry for revolution, a shout of freedom,
a call to arms, a ululating cry of grief –
and sometimes, the quietest thing,
a stillness whole and alone in a room chaotic with *Hosanna!*
The congregation, faces pressed to the ground,
adorn the feet of Jesus with tears
as angel tongues in mortal mouths
seek blessed assurance that Jesus is theirs.
And my mother sits or stands,
still in Presence.

Call Me Mara

My name is a thing of value, wasting
in the dark corners of our long years.

     In the dark corners of our long years
     I nurse regrets left over from our choices.

Someone must tend these regrets – leftover choices
will make you sick in the morning, love.

     I've been feeling sick in the morning, love.
     Bent over the toilet, spewing out the bitterness.

All these years, you've spewed out this bitterness
then called it the sacrifice of belonging.

     I held through everything but sacrificed our belonging.
     Building a home should not have done this.

Building a home should not have done this.
When you stripped my name off your tongue, I said Call me Mara.

The Language of Grief

The God my grandmother prayed to
and the Jesus I know are not the same.
I strive to infuse these words of prayer with
all the weight I have so I can lift the syllables in my kikuyu.

The weight of English on my tongue is too heavy for the
Ithe witũ ũrĩ igũrũ I need.

I fumble through The Lord's Prayer:
Ithe witũ ũrĩ igũrũ
Rĩĩtwa rĩaku rĩtheru rĩrotĩĩo –
Tell myself I will find the way –
Ũthamaki waku nĩũũke
reke wendi waku wĩkagwo gũũkũ thĩ.

I wrestle and fight for the tongue my mother taught to me.

My grandmother brought sacrifice to the Mugumo tree,
fig leaves a shade for the things she laid down.
Do the angels lay my prayers at your feet
the way Cucu pressed hers into the roots of the earth, Lord?

O ta ūrĩa gwĩkagwo kũu igũrũ,
give life to my mother tongue, I pray.

I pray to Jesus and call him Ngai.
Bury my hands in the earth and call him mūtũũria muoyo,
look to the mountains for help and say mũndeithia.

I pray and search for roots
and earth, and soil, and tree.
For truth, for God in all I see.

NOTES

'A Lending, Not a Giving' (p. 9) was first published by Bath Magg in their September 2019 issue.

'Call Me Mara' (p. 21) quotes author Tade Thompson in the opening line, "My name is a thing of value".

ACKNOWLEDGEMENTS

This short little pamphlet has been a labour of love that has taken many, many hours of work and many hands. I am thankful to my wonderful (and very patient!) editor, Emma Wright and the team at The Emma Press. I am grateful to the incredible women who love me and who do not shy away from sharing themselves, their stories, and their experiences with me. My sisters Lydia, Shermaine, Sijabulisiwe and Sylvia for their endless support and constant bearing up. Additional thanks to Fernanda Costa, Philemon and Benjamin Kinyanjui for their consistent support and encouragement. With thanks to my aunties, blood family and otherwise – thank you for your stories and your gracious willingness to guide me and answer my questions. My writing circle and creative family: Ashanti Wheeler-Artwell, Ashley Thorpe, Tade Thompson and Oquique.

Finally, to my incredible, resilient mama, Alice Wanjiku. You are the reason.

ABOUT THE POET

Rehema Njambi is a Kenyan-born, British-raised poet and writer whose work centres on womanhood, agency, faith and family. She has been a performance poet for over ten years and has performed broadly in the UK, Nairobi, and the US. In December 2020 she was longlisted for the Merky Books New Writers' Prize. She divides her time between Oxford and London. *This House* is her first collection.

ABOUT THE EMMA PRESS

The Emma Press is an independent publishing house based in the Jewellery Quarter, Birmingham, UK. It was founded in 2012 by Emma Dai'an Wright, and specialises in poetry, short fiction and children's books.

The Emma Press has been shortlisted for the Michael Marks Award for Poetry Pamphlet Publishers in 2014, 2015, 2016, 2018, and 2020, winning in 2016.

In 2020 The Emma Press received funding from Arts Council England's Elevate programme, developed to enhance the diversity of the arts and cultural sector by strengthening the resilience of diverse-led organisations.

Website: theemmapress.com
Facebook @theemmapress
Twitter @theemmapress
Instagram @theemmapress